Backed by Skiddaw and overlooking Derwent Water, Keswick is perfect for exploring the northern Lakes. Right: sunset over High Crag viewed from the Keswick landing stage.

- THE -
LAKE DISTRICT

Val Corbett

MYRIAD

Above: Ashness Bridge. Barrow Beck flows under this ancient packhorse bridge on the road to Watendlath.

Right: the Keswick Launch Company runs cruises around Derwent Water starting at the Keswick boat landing.

Left: stretching from the head of Derwent Water south to Seathwaite, Borrowdale is walled in by steep crags on all sides.

Right: the Borrowdale Show takes place in mid September. It is a wonderful opportunity to watch traditional sports, such as fell racing, tug-of-war and Cumberland and Westmorland wrestling.

Below: situated south of Keswick, the Castlerigg Stone Circle is one of Britain's most important neolithic monuments.

The view of Buttermere from the eastern end of the lake close to Gatesgarth Farm.

Above: looking across the Loweswater Valley to Crummock Water, sandwiched between the mountains of Grasmoor and Melbreak. In the far distance is the distinctive profile of Great Gable.

Above right: the side valley of Rannerdale leads away from Crummock Water.

Right: Bassenthwaite Lake, at the foot of Skiddaw. The word "lake" is included in its name – all the other lakes in the region are "meres", "tarns" or "waters".

The largest stretch of water in the Lake District, Windermere is the first stopping-off point for many visitors to Lakeland.

Left and below: Bowness. This quaint lakeside settlement is situated on the shores of Windermere.

Right: Troutbeck stretches for more than a mile along a side road off the Kirkstone Pass.

Surrounded by beautiful mountain scenery, Ambleside lies on the main road that runs between Keswick and Kendal.

Left: Bridge House on the Rydal Road in Ambleside dates from the 17th century. It straddles Stock Beck and is owned by the National Trust.

Right: the village of Rydal is famous for its association with the great Romantic poet, William Wordsworth. Rydal Mount, one of several characterful houses in the village, was the poet's home for the last four decades of his life.

The Langdale valleys are famous for their distinctive craggy windswept peaks – known as the Langdale Pikes.

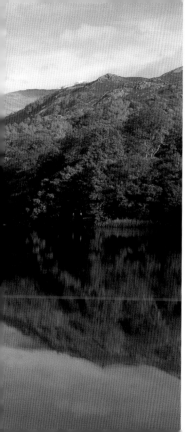

Left and above: with its strong literary connections, Grasmere is at the centre of some of Lakeland's most beautiful landscapes. William, Dorothy and Mary Wordsworth are buried in the Church of St Oswald. Dove Cottage lies in the hamlet of Townend on the outskirts of the village.

Famous for its steamers and lakeside walks, Ullswater is regarded by many as the most beautiful of the English lakes. This view from Glencoyne looks east towards the slopes of Place Fell, with Hallin Fell beyond.

Left: the Patterdale valley on the road between the Kirkstone Pass and Ullswater is a magnet for walkers. Towering above the small village is the Helvellyn mountain range; one of the most popular routes to the summit lies along the skyline.

Below: after walking along the Glencoyne shoreline of Ullswater, Dorothy Wordsworth wrote in her diary entry of 15th April 1802, "I never saw daffodils so beautiful..." William, her brother, included some of her description in his famous poem *I wandered lonely as a cloud*, also known as *Daffodils*.

Above: the 19th-century Ullswater steamers, *Raven* and *Lady*, will ferry you throughout the year to Howtown or Pooley Bridge. This bustling village lies close to the northern tip of Ullswater, about five miles south of Penrith.

Right: the Pooley Bridge landing stage.

Left: the spectacular Gothic ruin of Lowther Castle lies five miles south of Penrith on the eastern fringes of the Lake District.

Right: the unspoilt village of Hartsop is situated in a sheltered side-valley near Brothers Water at the northern foot of Kirkstone Pass. In the past the area was busy with mining, quarrying and milling. It is worth taking the short walk along the track to the Hayeswater Reservoir to see the impressive ruins of the watercourse and wheel-pit of the former Mires Head leadmine.

Left: the Haweswater reservoir was constructed in the 1930s by building the massive dam wall at Burbanks and enlarging the existing lake. The reservoir supplies Manchester with drinking water. Submerged beneath the water lies the old village of Mardale, drowned when the valley was flooded.

Below: Striding Edge. This dramatic route linking the summit ridge of Birkhouse Moor with the summit of Helvellyn is one of the most popular walks in the Lake District.

Below left: a wall runs along the 28-mile length of High Street, the course of a Roman road.

Coniston is at the heart of southern Lakeland. The area is rich in literary and sporting connections.

Left: Esthtwaite Water lies close to the villages of Near and Far Sawrey.

Right: Hill Top, the home of Beatrix Potter, is situated in Near Sawrey. The house, now owned by the National Trust, is open to the public. The author's furniture, china and watercolours are on display.

Left: the Old Man of Coniston dominates the landscape above the town. The slopes of the slate grey mountain are scarred by the legacy of old mineworkings – copper was extracted here for more than 500 years.

Right: Hawkshead is situated midway between Windermere and the northern end of Coniston Water. The town is a compact maze of buildings, dominated by the church of St Michael's and All Angels from its position high on Hawkshead Hill.

Left: a short, sharp climb from Hawkshead leads to the summit of Latterbarrow which gives dramatic panoramic views to the west across Hawkshead to the Coniston Fells.

Below: one mile north of Newby Bridge, Lakeside is a popular spot on Windermere and is busy with steam trains and pleasurecraft.

This dramatic photograph of Wasdale from Great Gable is taken from a vantage point close to the Westmorland Cairn, built in 1876 by two Westmorland brothers to mark what they regarded as the finest mountain viewpoint in the Lake District. Lying a few hundred yards south, and out of sight of the summit of Great Gable, it clings to the mountain's rim above a startling drop.

Left: Nether Wasdale is the tiniest of settlements and lies between Gosforth, Santon Bridge and Wast Water.

Below left: Hardknott Fort lies in a dramatic location below Hardknott Pass and just above Brotherilkeld Farm.

Below: Eskdale is a narrow valley linking the heart of the Lake District with the west coast. The view shows Brotherilkeld Farm and the Upper Eskdale valley from the slopes of Harter Fell.